A Scapegoat No More Forever

How to Heal from a Life of Being Scapegoated

Olivia Verbeck

Author's Note

This book discusses sensitive issues involving death, suicide, and the threat of suicide. These topics can be triggering for some. If at any point you become overwhelmed, please stop reading the book and seek help. If you are in the US, you can call the Suicide Prevention Lifeline 24/7 to speak with someone for free at 1-800-273-8255. If you are not in the US, please seek out resources available to you and get help. The purpose of this book is to educate and inform. The discussion of such topics is necessary to maintain safety and promote wellness for those facing the issues outlined in the book. Please read with care. Thank you.

Special dedication to my daughters Jacobi and Mia Verbeck for their never-ending love and support. You two are the favorite parts of my life.

As always, thank you to my Lord and Savior for all He has taught me and for loving me enough to save me.

BY OLIVIA VERBECK

How to Stop Chasing Rejection: Healing from Codependent Traits

The Relationship Trust Boundary Model: How to Take Your Rights Back

Have You Had Enough? How to Breakup with Your Toxic Cycle

I Can't Believe How Much This Hurts: How to Process a Breakup

For Jake,

I love you buddy.

CONTENTS

Chapter 7

Chapter 8

Chapter 9

Introduction

Scapegoats have been made to feel bad for so long, and as a result most of their behavior is driven by the need to prove they are good. Most believe it is their job to be of service to anyone who asks something of them. They often have no boundaries, get stuck in people-pleasing cycles, and have a strong fear of rejection. You may have been scapegoated in childhood or found yourself in a toxic relationship as an adult where you are or were scapegoated. Regardless of your scapegoat origins, the issues and ideas discussed in this book can help.

If you have struggled with toxic guilt, toxic shame, have a hard time letting go, or have found yourself approval seeking, this book is for you. Being scapegoated is painful. The effects can last a lifetime unless you make the decision to intervene and address the issues that stem from it. There is hope! Take the steps to learn how you were scapegoated as well as how to begin to address the underlying issues. It is possible to heal and overcome.

This book is designed to move you forward. I hope in the process you begin to understand you did not choose the role of scapegoat. It is not your job to uphold it. If at any time this book becomes too upsetting for you, please put it down and walk away to give yourself some time to process. If it is too upsetting, please seek help and find a local therapist in your area. You can use this book in therapy and walk through it with your therapist. Letting go is liberating. Learning to let go and not feel the toxic guilt afterward is what will allow you to keep moving forward, no more returning to old patterns. I am excited for you. I hope you reclaim your life and break free from this toxic role of *scapegoat*.

Part I

Bondage

Chapter 1

What is a Scapegoat

A scapegoat was created as a means for priests to deal with the sins of the people. The priest would place the sins of the people on the goat and then send the goat away. A scapegoat in a family is created out of a need for them to not have to carry what is wrong within the system. The scapegoat is made to feel they are fundamentally bad or broken. Everything is their fault because they never do anything right. They are manipulated into believing it is because of who they are, not because what the family is doing is wrong. Although the family as a unit upholds the role of the scapegoat, often, there is someone who assigns the role.

Scapegoats are made to feel less than. They are left out and labeled as the "bad one." You can read more about dysfunctional family roles including the role of scapegoat within an alcoholic family in Wegscheider-Cruse's book *Another Chance: Hope and Health for the Alcoholic Family* (Wegscheider-Cruse, 1981).

4

We will be using Wegscheider-Cruses' principles in a broader sense, beyond alcoholic families. We will be looking at how scapegoats can be created by a family, an entity, or an individual. You may have been scapegoated by just one family member, an individual, as well as a group. You can interchange "family" for the person or the people that scapegoated you.

Being a scapegoat is a lonely journey. Just like the goat that was sent out to wander alone in the wilderness, the scapegoat in a family feels like they are wandering all alone. The main interaction the scapegoat has in the family is when they are being labeled as "the bad guy". They were shamed regardless if they did anything wrong or not. If someone in the family says they did something wrong then they are treated as if they really did do something wrong. Being a scapegoat in a family means anyone can treat you as poorly as they want with little to no consequences. They can steal from you, hit you, lie about you, or leave you out and no one ever corrects the poor treatment. In fact, poor treatment of the scapegoat is often encouraged. What's more, the scapegoat is blamed for the treatment they receive.

If the scapegoat tries to speak up and report the poor treatment, they endure more accusations. They can be called, "big mouth", "cry baby", "disrespectful", "selfish", "annoying", etc. Also, they can be accused of "just wanting attention", or be told to, "stop lying." All of this is very confusing and painful for the scapegoat, especially in childhood. Their attacks can end in them being told, "just get out of my face", or "get out of here", so similar to the scapegoats from long ago. Taking the sin or shame on and then being sent away. They have become the secret keepers. Not only are they carrying everyone's shame, but they are also holding on to the secrets. Including the secret of how poorly they have been treated by their own family.

If you did not grow up in a dysfunctional family system, and you were instead scapegoated in a relationship, then the impact is similar. The scapegoat in the relationship is the one that is required to take on the blame for why the relationship is not working. They are not happy enough, not fit enough, too angry, or too needy. The scapegoat in a romantic relationship is the one putting in 1,000 times the effort and still being made to feel they are not doing "their part."

Scapegoats are so focused on not being seen as *bad*; they miss what is actually being done *to* them. The need to be good or to prove they are good is not their friend. The truth is, they were never bad. They were always good and always good enough. At the end of many relationships where someone was scapegoated, they look back and realize how much they actually gave and how little they actually got. The biggest shocker tends to come when they cannot imagine how they could not see it in the relationship. Being scapegoated feels so bad because someone is making you feel bad by constantly working on you and telling you how everything you are doing is not enough and then treating you poorly and blaming you for it. Anyone who spends enough time in this type of environment loses themselves and loses touch with reality.

Similarities:

In both a family system and a romantic relationship, the scapegoat tends to be the most mentally healthy. They tend to be more empathetic and relational. Scapegoats value relationships and they want to see others be happy and succeed. Scapegoats oftentimes are overly vulnerable. They tend to wear their hearts on their sleeves and give selflessly. The more they are scapegoated, the more they try to be "good" by denying self and performing tasks at their expense. Especially for those that do not value them.

The more the dysfunctional family or partner takes from them, the more they give and try to prove they are good and worthy of value. Scapegoats cannot see this will never get them value in the eyes of their abusers. Make no mistake about it, being scapegoated is abuse. You are being used in an attempt to satisfy someone else's need to get rid of their shame and guilt. The more shame and guilt the abusers feel the harder they scapegoat you.

Scapegoats tend to have a "guilty conscience". They worry they will get into trouble or get caught for doing something wrong even if they have done nothing wrong. Scapegoats go above and beyond in what they do. This is so they will *have* to be found innocent if anyone tries to accuse them of wrongdoing. This unhealthy fear of getting into trouble keeps scapegoats from standing up for themselves. This also prevents them from setting and holding boundaries, or relaxing and feeling good about themselves. Scapegoats tend to be on "high alert" and want to make sure they are doing more than everyone else. Being scapegoated sets you up to be a victim and to be re-victimized over and over. There are no boundaries, and they feel it is their job to be sure **everyone** else feels good.

After reading through this chapter, we can begin to see the traits of a scapegoat. Scapegoats are very capable and incredible people. They are full of pain and face constant rejection. Identifying what makes up a scapegoat is the first step. Next, let's look at how scapegoats are made.

Chapter 2

How Scapegoats are Made

We have already discussed *why* scapegoats are created. They are a means to deal with someone else's shame and or guilt. Now let's look at *how* they are created. There are four main tactics employed to create a scapegoat. They are:

1. Toxic guilt and toxic shaming
2. Smear campaign
3. Abandonment or the threat of abandonment
4. Death seed

Now, let's take a deeper look at each of these tactics so we can better understand what went into making a scapegoat.

1. Toxic guilt and toxic shaming

The scapegoat role involves shame, guilt, toxic shame and toxic guilt. These emotions are not only used to create the scapegoat role, the emotions become the primary emotions for the scapegoat.

9

This means they experience other emotions through shame and guilt, regardless if the emotion is pleasant or unpleasant. This begins to explain why scapegoats feel guilty for being happy, proud, pretty, handsome or any other pleasant emotion. This can lead to imposter syndrome. If a scapegoat begins to feel good about themselves, they are uncomfortable. They try to get their emotions in line by layering it with guilt in order to *feel* more comfortable. If they can convince themselves their success is not real, just luck, or that this person asked them out because they are just trying to be nice, then they can relax and get through the next moment.

The unpleasant emotions are also experienced and expressed as guilt and shame. Scapegoats may say things like, "I feel so bad" and express fear over unpleasant emotions, rather than saying they are sad, stressed or angry. It can also be difficult for scapegoats to hear what they have done wrong because they try so hard not to do anything wrong. They may have a stronger reaction to being told they are wrong when they have done something wrong more so than others. Not because they are egomaniacal, but because to them doing and being "good" is the difference between being loved and being left.

When we take on shame that belongs to another, it becomes toxic shame. This shame is now toxic because we cannot account for or correct the humiliating behavior of another. We can only correct our *own* behavior. In John Bradshaw's book, *Healing the Shame that Binds You,* he describes two types of shame. Healthy shame as "nourishing shame" and toxic shame as "life-destroying" shame (Bradshaw, 1988, p. 3). When we address what we have done wrong, the guilt can decrease. Part of the process of being scapegoated involves the transference of shame and or guilt. If someone is placing their guilt and shame upon you, rather than addressing their poor or bad behavior, you have become their scapegoat. Scapegoats have someone in their lives that does not own their own behavior and forces their shame and guilt upon the scapegoat. We will refer to this person as the scapegoat's **tormentor**. Eventually, the scapegoat just begins to pick up and carry the shame. In other words, over time, they do it to themselves in other relationships as well.

In a family system where there is a scapegoat, there is often a person in the family that is *shameless*. This family member does not feel shame over their own humiliating behavior. They are the ultimate victim, even when they are victimizing others in the home. They will only see what is being done to them. They will require sympathy from the family and transfer the shame to the scapegoat. The family system then reinforces the role upon the scapegoat, and will not hear or acknowledge the injustice being done to the scapegoat.

Scapegoats do not have a way to get rid of that toxic shame and guilt. They have been made to believe it is their shame to carry or their guilt to carry. They become burden bearers for the family, and if they do not do their job, they run the risk of being discarded. Scapegoats learn to get their value by how much they carry, take on, or give to the family. They are taught to do it without complaining.

Hopefully, you are beginning to see why scapegoats can become very shame based or guilt based. This results in feeling guilty all of the time or unworthy of anything good. This is how scapegoats blow up what they do wrong and down play or minimize what they do good, or right. Scapegoats grow up and rob themselves of opportunities, healthy relationships, and the unlimited progress that is available to them. Remember, scapegoats are incredibly healthy people. If given a voice, they would not allow toxic shame to be placed upon another. This is why you were chosen for a scapegoat, because you were strong, just and loving. You were a threat to the toxic family system from the beginning.

Scapegoats learn to work harder than others and ask for less than others. They have been programmed to believe it is their job to take on their part of the responsibility as well as others responsibilities. Scapegoats feel bad when things do not get done, although it was not their *job*. This is how scapegoats live out poor boundaries in life. They have not learned where they stop and start, or what to own and take on and what to leave for someone else to own. Scapegoats have a higher tolerance for poor treatment of themselves and a low tolerance for poor treatment of those who are less able. Scapegoats have a heart for those that are or have been oppressed. They root for the underdog because that is who they relate to.

In a family system where a scapegoat exists, the other members learn pretty quickly that no one wants to be the scapegoat. The members of the family system will be encouraged to "dump" on the scapegoat. Clear offenses will be done to the scapegoat. If the scapegoat does not just accept the poor treatment, they are shamed by the other family members until they do. This is very confusing for anyone to deal with. Clearly an offense just occurred, but if the scapegoat tries to express the poor treatment or how the poor treatment impacted them or how they feel, the family members will shame them. The family may say things like, "Why are you being so selfish?", "Oh don't be that way", or "my gosh you cannot take a joke, you are too sensitive!" Either way, the shame of the poor behavior becomes toxic shame for the scapegoat to carry. This leaves them with more toxic shame, because they have been shamed when they did nothing wrong.

The scapegoat has nothing to feel ashamed about. This is how scapegoats grow up and have a skewed sense of shame and guilt. Scapegoats feel it is somehow their job to fix or atone for others' bad behavior. Not only that, but scapegoats may feel guilt anytime they express an issue or a need. They were not allowed to express hurt feelings or needs because that was not part of the job description in the role within the family unit. This will cause issues in relationships later on in life. The family system is supposed to be a safe place for us to learn how to relate and connect in a healthy way. When the system does not allow this to take place, we struggle in the area of sharing and identifying needs. I know of scapegoats that do not know when they need to use the restroom until it is to the point where they almost cannot control it. Other scapegoats do not notice when they are hungry or have not eaten all day. They reach the point where they feel they are starving. They have been so busy all day trying to prove their worth. They are detached from their own body's basic needs. So how does being scapegoated get us to detach from our own needs? This leads us to the next tactic, the smear campaign. Let's take a look at what that is.

2. Smear campaign

Another factor that goes into making a scapegoat is being painted or labeled as "bad." To accomplish this, a smear campaign will be created to smear the name of the scapegoat. The family system has to sell the idea to the outside world that the scapegoat is "such a problem", or does such bad disrespectful acts. The scapegoat is talked about poorly in front of his or her face as well as behind their back. This is very shameful and humiliating for the scapegoat. This is an effective tactic that discredits them. The scapegoat is discredited before they get a chance to talk about the oppression, shameful acts, and often abuse that they are enduring. This way, by the time the scapegoat has a chance to speak, they just look like a trouble maker or a liar which is exactly the picture their family has painted. Next let's look at how withholding and abandonment can create a scapegoat.

3. Abandonment or the threat of abandonment

Abandonment can be either emotional or physical. Emotional abandonment is when someone may be physically next to you, but they are emotionally unavailable to you. Emotionally they are ice cold. If you hug them, they may get angry or not hug you back. They look *through* you and not *at* you. They will treat you as though you are invisible or not in the room. Your questions, concerns and affections are met with silence. They will not open up to you or with you. Emotional abandonment is effective in "training" a scapegoat.

Physical abandonment, on the other hand, is when you are left or sent away. This abandonment can happen in a moment often without warning. One-minute things may seem good and the next minute the other person is gone, or you find yourself somewhere alone and abandoned. Other times, there may be an escalation and then you end up abandoned. Regardless of which type of abandonment occurs or how it occurs, the impact is effective on a scapegoat. Lastly, we will look at something I like to call the death seed.

4. Death Seed

This is a heavy one. The death seed is planted into the scapegoat and it is watered any time the scapegoat confronts or tries to pull out of the toxic system. The death seed is a reminder of the tormentor's inevitable death. Their mortality is brought up to handcuff the scapegoat. The talk of a future death or the threat of a death disarms the scapegoat and places them back in harm's way.

There are those who are in the scapegoat's life who will try to use the death seed to get the scapegoat to stick around and accept punishment. The toxic guilt the death seed creates causes us to feel great fear around the torment's eventual death. Over time, this constant reminder of their coming death causes us to see them as fragile even when they are not. Who could confront or leave someone who is going to die? The talk of a future death is effective in getting us to focus on how it will be when they pass, or how precious our time is with them because they are only here for a short while. In truth, they will pass away someday because everyone is going to, even us. Does that mean we owe them our lives, our peace, our children, etc.? If you grew up where the death seed was planted, chances are it is still controlling you.

These tactics are all a form for psychological warfare. They attack your psyche. They are designed to break you down. Anyone who endures the abuse from being scapegoated breaks down eventually. The scapegoat is not allowed to leave. Any time the scapegoat has had enough and tries to leave, the family guilts them or begs them to stay or return. You can imagine how confusing this is for the scapegoat. The system or person only shows they care when they feel the scapegoat is fed up. The manipulation does not stop for the scapegoat. We have discussed families, now let's look at how a scapegoat is created in a romantic relationship.

In romantic relationships, scapegoats can still have the big four tactics used against them to create a scapegoat. Being shamed and guilted when the shame and guilt belong elsewhere, smear campaigns, abandonment, and the death seed. These tactics are effective in keeping the scapegoat bound and confused. The scapegoat is the trash can, the sin and secret keeper, and the punching bag.

A scapegoat will have the same role in a romantic relationship. Their partner will not be capable or willing to pick up their own shame. They will find a scapegoat to be with, or they will slowly create a scapegoat over time. If you were scapegoated in childhood, it would be more familiar for you to entertain and engage with someone that scapegoats you. If you were not scapegoated in childhood, then throughout the relationship you will experience the painful and confusing reality that scapegoats face. It will feel like you are trying to love someone who hates you.

In addition to the four main tactics used within a family system, your partner may use a handful of tactics in the relationship to scapegoat you. The following is a list of new behaviors that are common when creating a scapegoat in a relationship. There are no excuses for these behaviors. Each of these behaviors are tactics of manipulation and do not belong in healthy, loving relationships.

1. Double standard - Someone has a double standard when they ask you not to do something and then you find them doing exactly what they have forbidden you to do. They may demand you do something they themselves will refuse to do. Double standards will oftentimes have a layer of guilt laced with it. This is part of what makes it so infuriating when you come across a double standard. Here is an example. Let's say your partner says they need your passwords so they can feel safe with you, but after you give up your passwords, they refuse to give you theirs. When you become outraged and demand they give you their password as well, they give you a guilt trip for not trusting them. When you point out to them that they have your passwords, they flip it on you. They explain away the double standard by implying you are "bad" therefore, they need your passwords. They also imply they are not bad therefore; you do not need theirs. They are scapegoating you while claiming sainthood.

2. Gaslighting – The idea of gaslighting comes from the 1944 film *Gaslight* where a woman is manipulated into questioning her own reality (Cukor, G., 1944). This is what gaslighting

does. It causes you to question your own reality. Over time you detach from your senses. You will deny what you see and instead only believe what is being told to you in the moment. This causes debilitating self-doubt and allows you to stay abused. We cannot deal with what we cannot acknowledge. Gaslighting forces our eyes shut and opens up our ears.

3. Dismissing – This occurs when your partner is dismissive of your wants and needs or of you physically. They may refuse to acknowledge your presence. If you are speaking, they may wave their hand in a motion for you to "be gone" or to "get out." Being dismissed can instantly make you feel like you have less rights and are less important. Any time you think of a scapegoat, imagine the scapegoat that took on all the sin and then was sent away. That is what being dismissed feels like. It feels bad and is a lonely place to be in.

4. Labeled the "Bad Guy" – No one likes a bad guy. Everyone has permission to treat them poorly. If you have ever gone around someone that your partner knows and they are treating you poorly, you may be confused by this and think they do not like you for *no reason*. The hard truth is, your partner may be painting you as the bad guy to them and that may be why they do not like you. You may have been painted in a bad light. Instead of asking the person if we have done something to offend them, we typically go to our partners to try to understand why their family, friends or co-workers do not like us. A better question is: if the friends and family know us

through our partner, what has our partner been saying about us that might cause them to not like us?

Much like the first four tactics, these last four can also occur within a family system, they are not exclusive to romantic relationships. Being on the other end of these behaviors is very painful and confusing. Trying to love someone and be close to someone who is using these tactics on you leaves you in the dark. They are blaming you for why they are treating you poorly. Oftentimes the more you try to get their acceptance and the more you do for them, the worse they treat you. It is not normal to have the one you love treat you like you are stupid, bad, or invisible.

Chapter 3

Issues Scapegoats Face

When it comes to facing issues, scapegoats seem to have some in common. This is why learning what it means to be scapegoated is so powerful. You no longer feel alone. You no longer have to feel bad or the need to prove your innocence. Knowing others have also gone through this can help you to feel less alone. Others were also sent off to wander alone. It wasn't just you. There are others that didn't deserve it either.

Coming out of this blanket of shame and guilt makes what has been going on visible. It can show how you have been reacting as a result of the toxic shame and toxic guilt. You may not relate to every one of the issues a scapegoat faces, or each one may be spot on for you. Either way, please know you are not broken or a terrible person. You are a person who was manipulated because you loved someone that could not or would not deal with their own shame. Nothing is wrong with you. You are an incredible loving person and that is why you were chosen for a scapegoat. You are actually incredibly strong to have survived what you have gone through. So, take a breath and let's dive into some of these issues.

Each of these issues stem from the toxic shame that has been placed on the scapegoat.

1. Need to prove you are good or worthy
2. Explain or defend yourself
3. People pleasing behavior
4. Victimization

Let's go through each one of these and break them down.

1. The need to prove you are good or worthy

Having your name smeared in the mud does something to your confidence and self-worth. Being talked "bad" about has a strange way of dehumanizing you and making you feel invisible. For anyone who has never endured an entire smear campaign, they more than likely will not understand the depth of the damage that it can do. It is not simply enough to decide, "you know the truth, don't even worry about it", especially if you were raised this way. The shame and embarrassment you feel when you walk into a room, thinking everyone is thinking you are bad is debilitating. Having to go and face those that have listened to someone who has bashed you is beyond embarrassing. Especially, when the one doing the bashing is your mother, father or spouse. Each of these roles in your life is supposed to support, protect, and love you. Who would believe they would lie to the extent they do especially for no reason. Therefore, they must be telling the truth, right? The person smearing your name discredits you before you ever have a chance to even learn what is being said about you. You are walking into a well laid plan.

The smear campaign completes its job by sealing your mouth shut. You learn early on that the more you try to prove your innocence or argue that you did nothing wrong, the more pathetic or guilty you somehow become. You learn to just take it. The pathetic feeling is often worse than the shame. In an effort to compensate for this, you go to work proving you are good. You wait for that, "Sorry, I always thought you were bad, but you're actually ok." Or the moments when someone approaches you and says, "You are a really good daughter, I hope she realizes it." When scapegoats get these confirming statements, they just try to carry on and not engage, because again, they know that if they start to engage, they will somehow end up pathetic yet again. So, they do not share their experience. They don't open up to the truth of what is really happening. It's the shame and the toxic shame that keeps their mouth shut. If you are or were a scapegoat, it can feel like there is no winning. However, having this validation that you are worthy or good even for a moment means so much.

As a result of having your name smeared into the mud, on top of learning that opening your mouth leaves you feeling more pathetic, you are left to allow your actions to speak for themselves. As a result, you may begin to prove your worth with your actions while having no boundaries. This looks like you going above and beyond for anyone who asks something of you. Never asking for a return favor. Never telling someone no. This need to prove you are not the horrible things that were said about you drives your behavior, and can ultimately control your life. The worry of having someone believe you are bad, can outweigh your needs, wants, and limitations. You may struggle to understand that you are allowed to say no. You may also struggle in confronting someone for their bad behavior, or to have needs that you express. Being scapegoated confuses all of this for you especially in relationships.

Scapegoats tend to be very valuable. They go above and beyond without much supervision. They have learned the art of meeting needs by stepping in and stepping up. They know how to make themselves valuable and how to not have to be "asked twice" to do something. Scapegoats try to feel safe by showing they are good or worthy. This leaves them vulnerable and may put them at risk of further scapegoating. They are forever in fear of being scapegoated and sent away or abandoned and this drives the people pleasing behavior.

2. Explaining or defending yourself

Anyone who spends a period of time being victimized will get used to defending and explaining themselves. Once you have a smear campaign run on you, you lose your privacy. No longer having privacy, you may not know what to share and what not to share. So, on top of feeling the need to prove you are "good", you now feel you owe any and everyone an explanation for what you do and do not do. This creates issues with boundaries. Trying to prove we are good with explaining our every move leaves us almost pleading or begging. This makes us feel desperate for acceptance. It is because we do not understand our right to privacy. We feel we *have* to answer a question just because it was asked.

You will find scapegoats explaining what they are doing and why they are doing it. Even with things that are no one's business. When you come across it, it can be shocking. As adults we make our own decisions and decide what we will and will not do. What we will or will not have. However, scapegoats experience a different reality even in adulthood.

Scapegoats have been abused and neglected. They have been trained that their job is to make sure those around them feel "good" while they feel bad. This teaches someone to make their decisions based on if someone else will be happy with what they do or not. A healthy adult will consider the impact their decisions have on those in their lives, but ultimately, they make decisions based upon their own value system. Not based on how someone else will feel. This leads us to the next issue, people pleasing.

3. People pleasing behavior

Making decisions based on how someone else feels creates a people pleaser. You may find yourself going along or changing who you are to fit the person or people you are with just to try to make them happy. You do this so you do not get left or miss out. You may even hate this behavior in you. This can cause you to step outside of your morals and say and do things that you do not agree with. Trying to gain favor for no other reason than to avoid being abandoned. You stop looking at the quality of the relationship and instead solely focus on if there is a relationship. It is the presence of the relationship that derives all meaning, rather than what the relationship offers you or the quality of the relationship.

This can set you up to be used. It will keep you from setting boundaries and saying "no more." You can have a great deal of anxiety while you are with someone and feel uncomfortable. You may even dread being with that person. However, anytime they ask you to hang out with them, or they want to talk to you on the phone you do not say no. It can feel as though your job is to please them. It is all about them and their schedule, wants, and needs. Even something as simple as saying, "I need to go now", to get off the phone can create increased levels of anxiety. This can lead to avoidance in relationships. Feeling fine outside of a relationship and then stuck or miserable while in one.

The fear of being scapegoated and ultimately abandoned causes us to people please instead of having honest direct communication. Again, being scapegoated also breads people pleasing behaviors because we do not want people to see that we are bad. We learn to lay our true selves aside. When you are scapegoated, you learn that everything you want, need and are, is wrong. Over time, that critical judgement causes you to set yourself aside and eventually you lose touch of what it is that you value. You have become someone else's shame no longer feeling like a person. We begin to get value by being valued by someone else. Someone who is truly interested in you will not want you to people please with them, they want to know *you*.

The only problem is by the time you have endured the amount of scapegoating that goes into creating this behavior, you may have lost sight of who you are.

4. Victimization

Once you have been scapegoated for an extended period of time, you may find yourself looking for someone to have your back. Someone to protect or fight for you. You may surround yourself with dangerous people and recruit them to protect you. We can do this by telling of our past or current victimization. This is an issue, because often this can become how we relate and connect to other people. We establish relationships based on how we were treated in the past. We tell someone our victimization story over and over again. What's more, we may make more out of new problems than what really exists or what has occurred.

Rather than having an issue with someone, we may feel the need to make ourselves the victim and someone else a terrible person to show just how innocent we are. This is still being driven by the old smear campaigns. We want to make it very clear that we have done nothing wrong and that everything is the other persons' fault. When we do this, we can become a "problem starter" in our relationships. This can interfere with our ability to get help and heal when we are victimized because we make the entire thing about our innocence rather than getting help for what has happened to us.

Take work for example. If I am at work and an issue arises, rather than confronting the issue, I may go to someone else trying to recruit them to protect me. I don't want to be scapegoated or have a smear campaign run on me. I get busy early on explaining what was done to me, showing myself to be innocent. My focus is more so on showing that I am the victim so I won't be the bad guy and end up abandoned. I care more about being innocent than I do about what actually happened to me. This fear of the smear campaign will have me victimizing myself over a misunderstanding. I will inadvertently cause more issues for myself than the initial issue caused me.

One other contributing factor that goes into victimization can be when you start to find a place or person where you feel like you fit in. You may begin to feel safe enough to open up and share. Once you tap into yourself, you will find lots of past victimizations that you have endured. As you begin to try to share with the other people in your life, you can find yourself talking often about what happened to you or what someone has done to you. There may be years of pent up hurt you have never spoken about or processed. So, when it begins to come out you keep regurgitating it or recycling it. Finally finding the freedom and courage to tell your truth is liberating in the beginning. Over time however, it can become part of your narrative or your story. Some may get tired of hearing it and eventually target you as well, only adding to your victimization. This can become a vicious cycle that you find yourself in. It can follow you from job to job and relationship to relationship. We definitely do not want this to become part of our identity, experiencing this is incredibly painful.

When we are used to being victimized, we can go into crisis mode quickly more so than those that have not been victimized. A misunderstanding is more likely to be seen as an attack, or an issue can become perceived as rejection. Your response can come across as though you have a "chip on your shoulder."

Victimization makes us hyper aware, and we can look for threats. We may see threats where there aren't any. This makes us defensive and overly sensitive. Just like a physical wound is sensitive to touch, so are emotional wounds. We can become sensitive because emotionally we are inflamed from a life of being agitated where we have been emotionally poked and prodded. This makes for miserable relationships, again both at work and at home. What's more, if you are being victimized by being scapegoated, you are not allowed to share how you are feeling. You don't get to be the victim around those that support you being scapegoated or those that are scapegoating you. This is an issue for two reasons:

1. You can get "inflamed." Sharing your pain and your experience helps the swelling go down and the wound can then heal. If you cannot share your truth, then the wound doesn't heal, it only gets more irritated and sensitive.

2. You do not learn *how* to share your feelings. This is one of the reasons why when you do finally begin to share, you find yourself sharing the same things over and over. Still not much healing is occurring because it doesn't go anywhere. We need to learn how to share, and that takes practice as well as a safe place to learn how to practice. This is where a support system comes into a play. Having a support system is vital to our healing. We will discuss that more in a later chapter.

Looking over the issues that scapegoats face can bring up feelings of anger, resentment, confusion, sadness, etc. There is no wrong emotion. Looking back over this list makes me sad. I sit here and think, "What a waste of time. What is all of this for and who was this benefiting?" I think a larger question is… HAVE YOU HAD ENOUGH? Are you done being scapegoated? Are you done with having no rights, no voice, and no say? Are you done carrying the family shame? Are you done being made to feel bad and taking poor treatment from anyone at any time while trying your hardest to maintain these dysfunctional relationships? If so, take a deep breath and let's look at how to be a *scapegoat no more, forever*.

Part II

Breaking Free

Chapter 4

Letting Go of the Fear of Abandonment

Many of the behaviors of the scapegoat are driven by the fear of rejection. No one likes rejection but scapegoats can be crippled it. The true fear, however, is the fear of abandonment. Scapegoats feel that if you reject them, then you are going to leave them. They do not like being left or being sent away. It is this fear of abandonment that prevents them from letting go even when things get toxic. The scapegoat becomes more concerned with someone staying, than how they are being treated.

Growing up and being abandoned, or being with a partner who walks out can be devastating. When you are left or left out, you feel bad. You feel like you are the worst person on the planet and you are so bad that no one can be around you. When we begin to wake up and realize we were only abandoned when we tried to stand up for what was right, things start to look different. We begin to find our strength. Here is the secret.

1. You have to be willing to let go of those that do not value you.
2. You have to be willing to let go of those that refuse to stop punishing you, or those that demand you accept punishment from someone else. That person is not showing you love. They are not even thinking about you as a person with feelings and rights. You are a scapegoat that needs to keep carrying the shame so they can maintain the status quo and keep on with their lives.
3. You have to be willing to let go of those who continue to paint you or portray you as the bad guy and scapegoat you.
4. Be willing to let go of anyone that expects you to condone abuse. This can be the abuse of another, or if they expect you to allow someone to abuse you or treat you poorly.

I realize this is easier said than done. Especially if you have spent a significant period of time being shamed and scapegoated. The toxic shame over time causes you to question your ability to correctly place blame where it goes. You will blame yourself or make excuses for their poor behavior because that is how you have been living.

In a dysfunctional relationship or in a dysfunctional family system, the one that tries to talk about the abuse or confront the abuse is the one that is abandoned. The whistleblower is the one that gets heaps of shame. Over time this teaches us that blowing the whistle or outing abuse is wrong. In fact, it is worse than what the abuser is doing. Scapegoats need to go through a process of unwinding and straightening out all of the twists and turns that the toxic shame has made of their thoughts. Really understanding what abuse is and what makes up a healthy relationship is vital for a scapegoat. Once you understand these two areas, letting go of those that will not address their abusive or manipulative behavior gets easier and easier. We are letting go of the abusive unjust behavior, not just cutting people out of our lives. We will cover this more in Chapter 8.

The hope is that we reach a point where we will not accept abusive or unjust behavior towards us or anyone else. We will only accept loving, supportive and healthy behavior. That is not too much to ask. This needs to be the minimum we accept. Anyone who thinks it is your job to take on the shame and then keep your mouth shut while you are lied about, bullied, hit, ripped off and abandoned, is not someone I would want in my corner. That sounds like what an enemy does to you, not what siblings, parents, friends or spouses are supposed to do to each other.

This does not mean that you have to let someone go. You may decide to set some boundaries in place first. There may come a time when you decide they ultimately do not belong in your life. The point is, we cannot begin to address and talk about the abuse, as long as we are still afraid to let go. Once we begin to make peace with the fact that we may lose this person if we open our mouths, that is when we begin to find our strength. This is why the willingness has to come first. If we really think about it, why would we want someone in our lives that will not allow us to tell what is happening to us or what we are afraid of? That is not a real relationship. Relationships have exchanges. Exchange of emotions, thoughts and of ourselves. If someone is only flowing one way, that is a oneship, not a relationship.

Anyone that is abusive to you or expects you to accept or take abuse is not a safe person for you. This can be hard to hear and even more difficult to accept especially if you have endured years of abuse. You were not trained to see the poor treatment. You were trained to only watch how you were treating others.

All of this applies to a romantic relationship. The willingness to let your partner go if they will not address the poor treatment is a great place to start. We can even let this be our filter. If we talk about the scapegoating behavior, and that person exits our life because we tried to bring it up… then good riddance. Remember, why would we want to be in the presence of those that expect us to take poor treatment and keep our mouths shut? Now that we have discussed the idea of being willing to let go of those that demand we stay scapegoats, let's look at another important point that will continue to help us stop being scapegoats.

Chapter 5

Stop Defending and Explaining Yourself

As we discussed previously, scapegoats explain and defend themselves when they do not need to. This comes from the need to prove their innocence because of the smear campaigns they have endured. Scapegoats have also been made to feel that they "asked" for the treatment they received. We can see how this treatment creates a need for someone to be innocent all the time and can also begin to develop a guilty conscience. Scapegoats feel they "owe" any and everyone an explanation when in reality they do not.

If you struggle with this, you will continue to feel victimized and seek validation for how you feel and act. This makes you vulnerable each time you explain yourself because you are opening yourself up and looking for approval. We are looking for approval when we do this because we are waiting for the outcome of what we are saying. Is the other party going to see we are innocent or are they going to side with those that say horrible things about us and shame us too? Once we realize we do not need someone to save us and that we can stand up for ourselves with no explanation, we begin to find our strength.

This can seem tricky. What is the difference between stating what you have been through as fact versus sharing what happened to you with the hopes that you will be believed? It's the agenda. If you catch yourself pushing an agenda, you may be falling into old patterns that leave you feeling helpless, shameful, and victimized. If you instead make statements and use your voice to speak the truth and then leave it, you will notice you walk away feeling more confident. This does not mean you need to share all of your truth. You decide how much you share. This does not mean you are trying to pull a "poor me" or that you were not truly victimized. If you were or are a scapegoat, you have absolutely been victimized and it is incredibly daunting and painful to deal with. Remember, this portion is about moving forward and learning how to share your truth without falling into an old role. It is not about not sharing your truth. This is about learning how to share your truth in a new way that does not set you up for further victimization.

Part of the freedom comes when we begin to understand what we share and who we share with is up to us and is our business only. Our past experiences are **our** stories. We carry the scars, keep the memories and hold the pain, so it's ours. It is not for someone else to have access to unless we decide it is. Just because someone has an opinion on our lives, or tries to make us "bad" does not mean they deserve to hear our story.

We have rights. The right to say no and to say, "That is not something I am willing to talk about right now." Scapegoats often undergo interrogations, so they are used to being put under the "lamp" and being drilled with questions. Being made to feel it is their job to answer no matter how personal or private it may be. Scapegoats are not allowed privacy. Any part of them can be used and exploited at any time. If they try to defend themselves it gets worse for them. This means, they never learned how to protect themselves in a healthy way. Instead, they were punished for protecting themselves instead of being respected. This can cause problems in relationships at work, church, friendship groups, etc. This causes the scapegoat to come across as very defensive. Having never been given the respect to their right to privacy, they may feel that they need to come out swinging and feel a strong need to protect themselves. This is why it is so powerful when a scapegoat learns their rights come from within them, not from individuals on the outside. Let me say it again. Your rights come from within, not from those outside of you. You do not need to wait or be dependent on someone to give or approve of your rights. You already have your rights inside of you, you need to exercise your rights if you want to have some.

This means we can hold our boundaries and exercise our rights rather than feeling like we need to "fight" others for our rights. No more waiting to see if they will think of us and give us some. Once we realize we have rights and begin to exercise them, the defensiveness goes down. Now we are not engaging in toxic boundaries. Otherwise, it comes across as though we are the ones making the problems with others or that we have a "chip" on our shoulder.

I am hoping this is starting to hit home. Not only for what may have been done to you, or the impact it has had on you, but also to give you some ideas on where to begin your healing journey. Here are some safeguards or guides for scapegoats when dealing with relationships moving forward.

1. Only have close relationships with those that respect you. This can be a tricky one for scapegoats because they were either raised in a home where they were never given respect, or they have been manipulated into believing they do not deserve respect. Someone who has respect for you thinks of you and your needs and they respect them. They listen to you when you speak. They don't call you names. They do not put you down in front of others or behind your back. They don't talk down to you or deny you the credit that you deserve. They are true to their word. They do what they say and say what they do. They don't lie to you. We all have reasons for what we do, but remember, it does not matter why someone disrespects you. What matters is if they respect you or not. No matter how horrible their childhood or their last relationship was, there is never an excuse for abuse or disrespect. If someone does not have respect for you, then they do not get to be close to you.

2. Learn to have varying degrees or levels of relationships. Not everyone is either in or out. We can have several different types

of relationships with the different people in our lives. Not every person you meet or get to know is going to be a "friend". Not every friend is going to be a best friend. Not every coworker is going to end up a friend. They may just continue to be a coworker and never move beyond that. Or someone may remain a friend but never become a best friend. This does not mean that we have failed at these relationships in our lives. It just means that this is the relationship we have with that specific individual and it is okay. When we allow the relationships that come into our lives to develop with time, it makes for a less bumpy road. If we only have three categories for people such as: friend, partner, or enemy, then when we meet someone new those are the only options we have for them. We need to expand the categories we have for the people in our lives. It frees us up to just enjoy our experiences instead of stressing about them.

3. Go slow in your relationships. Get to know someone before you call them a friend or relate with them on a friend level. Go to coffee, different events, or maybe to dinner a few times. Get to know their character. Scapegoats have been surrounded by those that are critical of them. Those that do not respect them or value them. They also have a history of being used by the people in their lives. Use these traits as measures to see if you want to be friends with someone new that you meet. Are they critical of you or others? Do they see the value in you and reflect that to you? Do they say things like, "You are really talented", or "You are so creative!", or "It's nice being around

you"? You will also want to watch out for love bombing or fake praise. Someone giving you way too much praise or giving you compliments you know you have not earned. You may want to dial back and give yourself some space from that person. Going slow keeps you at a distance where you can see who they are. After a period of time, you can decide based on what you have seen and how you feel when you are around them if you want to be their friend. Even then, you need to decide how close of a friend you want to be with them.

Learning our protection comes from within us when we begin to exercise our rights, helps us to not have to explain ourselves or get caught up in defending ourselves. Explaining and defending ourselves makes us feel small and at the mercy of those in our lives whether at work or at home. The reality is, we were small once, but we are not any longer. Exercise your rights. Decide how much you want to share with someone and if you find yourself being interrogated, don't engage. It doesn't have to be a scene or require you to fight. It can simply be a statement of whatever it is you want to share. Let's look at an example.

Mark is 23. He has been the family scapegoat his entire life. His older brother James feels it is his place to control Mark and to make him answer anytime Mark is not doing what mom wants him to do. Mark recently missed a family event and has been dreading going back home because of the guilt trips and shame he will face. Mark has a history of either fighting back and feeling pathetic afterward, or he just does whatever his mother wants him to whether he wants to do it or not. Sometimes the guilt trips and shame he faces are worse than just going along with her. This time, however, Mark really did not want to go, so he chose to do something else. He was not sure what to say, so he said nothing and just did not show up or respond to his controlling family's texts. Now it is Thanksgiving Day, and he is dreading facing his family.

James- Hey Mark, nice of you to show up. We all texted you and called the other day when we came to mom's where were you? Mom was really upset. She's really lonely and needs all of us here with her as much as we can.

Pause- Normally, Mark would turn red-faced and start to feel like the "bad" scapegoat for hurting his poor mother. He would either defend or explain himself, but not today. Mark has already made the decision that he will not be doing either one of those options. Now he must decide how much of his truth, of where he was and why he did not join the family the other day, he wants to share. Mark thinks about the truth. "I just didn't want to come, so I could be ignored or made fun of and have to sit here for 4 or 5 hours after the movie so I decided to go for a hike instead and it was great." This is the truth. Mark knows James is only interested in the truth to the extent that he can use it against him for the purpose of guilting him as a means to regain control over Mark. So instead, Mark replies the following:

Mark- Oh hey James! Sorry to hear mom is sad and lonely, I am glad you guys were able to be here. I had other plans.

James- Oh, so you had other plans isn't that great?

Mark- Yes, I did but I am glad you were able to come.

James- Don't you think we had other plans too? Don't you care about mom?

Mark- What?

James- Don't you care about mom?!

Mark- Yes

James- Then how can you just not come?

Mark- I had other plans. Hey, I am going to grab seconds. (Gets up and walks away to get more food)

When someone is trying to scapegoat you, they may try different angles to paint you as the bad guy. If you do not engage you can see how what they are saying becomes more and more ridiculous. The absurdity in what they are saying is not shown when you engage and take on the family shame. You just end up the bad guy. Notice how Mark says few words and repeats himself. In reading his response he appears to be almost bulletproof and yet he does not overtly come across as defensive or as if he is threatened by James in any way. The "old" Mark would have caved to the pressure of the shame and the fear that James would walk away from him. Mark now knows that he can let go of this close toxic relationship if James does not stop trying to shame and control him.

Also, notice how Mark validated what James is saying. Mom is sad. Mark acknowledged that in his response but he did not own his mother's feelings. She is allowed to be sad. That is not Mark's fault or his problem to fix. Everyone gets sad. That does not mean Mark does not feel bad because she is sad, or that he doesn't empathize with her. It just means that he is not going to be responsible for how she feels. She is responsible for how she feels. When we are learning to not defend or explain ourselves, validation is a great tool to use at the beginning of your response. This is the "sorry to hear mom is sad" part. As you begin to practice making statements rather than defending or explaining, try to first validate a portion of what they have said, then give your response and make it brief. "I had other plans."

One new idea for scapegoats is the fact that they can leave or walk away especially if they are receiving poor treatment. Scapegoats are not used to exercising their freedom. As an adult, embracing the reality that they can leave, walk away or choose not to answer a question is a radical idea. Scapegoats will not naturally have these options as possibilities because this has not been their reality. It is important to realize that as an adult, you are in charge of you. Solely you, alone, just you. You get to choose where you go and who you allow in your life. You decide what you will discuss and what you will not discuss. There is not a person or relationship that is more important than the relationship you have with yourself. You have every right to advocate and set boundaries with others.

Scapegoats often feel fear and panic when they think about not complying with the poor treatment. There is a struggle we face as we begin to learn how not to accept scapegoat treatment. Part of that struggle is either being very defensive or feeling like you owe everyone an explanation for your decisions. As you navigate some of these new ideas, it is important to be patient with yourself. Realizing that you are not going to do any of this perfectly. Over time, you will find your strength and find tactics that work best for you. Check-in with yourself after you exercise your rights and see how you are feeling. The feeling you get after tells you where you are at and also if you feel good about the way you handled a situation.

Remember, if you are defending or explaining yourself, you may be falling back into your scapegoat role. Practice exercising your rights and stop explaining yourself to everyone. Next, we will discuss how to deal with the death seed that was planted to keep you stuck.

Chapter 6

Plucking Out the Death Seed

This is a tough one. The death seed is so effective in achieving its' designed purpose that oftentimes you do not realize the grip it has on you. It is not limited to just your tormentor's future death, the stress over how their funeral will go can keep you in a scapegoat role. What will people say if you do not go? What will people say if you do go? Is setting boundaries and going no contact really worth all of this stress and division? All of this is coming from the death seed.

We have been conditioned to see our tormentors as fragile and manipulated into believing that not doing what they want will kill them. This means it is our fault if they die. This is how we can begin to feel guilty because they are going to die someday. It is difficult to understand how crippling the death seed is unless you have had one planted in you. So, what does the death seed look like? How is it planted in us? Here are a couple of examples of how a family system or a romantic relationship plants the seed.

Tormentor: Well maybe you all will be happier when I am dead!

Family: (stops confronting) That's not true! We love you! Nothing will be the same without you!

Tormentor: If you leave, I will kill myself

Partner: I promise you; I will never leave you

Tormentor: I have just had it! No one is happy, I am just going to kill myself and then everyone can just go about their business and just live perfect lives!

Family: We are happy, look we won't fight. We'll be good children. We're sorry please don't kill yourself!

Imagine the impact this threat has on a child. This can keep a child up all hours of the night fearing their tormentor's impending death. In a relationship, this makes the partner's heart drop any time there is a fight, or a late text response and especially if they think of leaving. So how do we deal with the death seed once it has been planted? In truth, it stays in you from relationship to relationship. You may fear the death of every person you connect with. This is different from being grateful or mindful of the time you have with someone. The death seed keeps you from setting and holding healthy boundaries. The fear of another's death trumps all abuses and needs.

Knowing where this fear comes from is liberating. The understanding that this seed was planted in us to control and manipulate us begins to lessen the grip on us. Recognizing that we will also pass one day, makes the tormentor's death less special if you will. Once that grip loosens you can get yourself free of it. So how do we deal with someone who tries to threaten us with their death? Let's take a look at some tools we may need.

First off, we always take the threat of suicide seriously. If someone threatens to take their life, we try to get them help. You can call your local suicide hotline, the police or go to your local Emergency Room, to name a few resources. If you live in the United States, you can call the Suicide Prevention Lifeline 24/7 to speak with someone for free at 1-800-273-8255. I do not recommend ignoring someone who is threatening to take their life or just trying to help them yourself. Seek support. If they threaten you or beg you not to tell, this is not safe for you or them.

Use your judgement and also tell someone close to you. This can be a trusted family member, friend or a therapist if you are seeing one. Once someone has threatened to take their life it can begin to control you. You may find yourself consumed with the fear of their death. If they choose to take their life it will be devastating and painful. It will not be your fault. We never tell someone they should just kill themselves; we take their threat seriously and try to get them help. We do not allow the fear of their self-harming threat or behavior to control us. We are not in charge of them, we can only listen and try to get them help. Seek professional help in your local area to deal with this but do not allow it to force you to comply with demands or threats.

If you have lost someone to suicide or had someone threaten you with suicide, I am so sorry. The shame and guilt associated with suicide can be unbearable. Individuals that have taken their life tend to have a history of threatening suicide. This is why we take each threat seriously. It may be a tactic of manipulation but it may very well be a cry for help. Try to get them help, be safe and get yourself help as well. You may not have access to a suicide hotline, but you can go online and see the help available to you as well as contacting your local hospital for options and resources. If this is something that is a current part of your life, I would encourage you to find and utilize resources today, do not wait.

All in all, the way we deal with the death seed is to realize that everyone is going to pass. Someone does not get to control you or guilt you because they are not immortal. We take suicide seriously and although we do not allow it to control us, we do try to get those in our lives help if they threaten to take their lives. This is a heavy topic and so many scapegoats that I personally know have dealt with it in some form or fashion and they do not know what to do with it. If this portion was too heavy for you, please take a break. If it stirred up any unresolved trauma, please seek a local therapist or support group in your area. Same rules for seeking help apply to you too. If you find yourself having thoughts of not wanting to be "here" anymore, or wanting to kill yourself, please get help. You can go to your local emergency room, find a therapist in your area and share with a safe person you trust. You deserve help.

Now that we have looked at how to break free, we need to look ahead to new life. What does new life mean? What does it take to create a new life and what will it take to embrace a new life? Take some deep breaths, stretch, and let's take a look at what new life can mean for us.

Part III

New Life

Chapter 7

Create a Support System

Most scapegoats do not have a support system. They tend to have a trail of toxic "friendships" where they have been hurt and disappointed. Relationships exhaust scapegoats because they are drawn to and draw in those that take from them and shame them. Scapegoats tell you some "weird" stories about what their "friends" have done to them. They draw individuals who seem to always have a big deal going on in their life and the scapegoat is there 100% percent of the time. Yet, when the scapegoat is in crisis, their friends are unavailable or will make it much worse by being dismissive and then shaming them.

Scapegoats face specific barriers when building a support system. One barrier is not knowing how to fully share their story. Remember, scapegoats are really good at helping others with their needs. They are not great at sharing *their* own needs. Scapegoats are filled with shame, and shame keeps your mouth shut. Oftentimes, the people in the scapegoat's life are not aware of what they are going through.

For scapegoats it is not about what is wrong with you, it is about what happened to you. This in and of itself is difficult because scapegoats have been convinced of their role for so long, they cannot clearly see all that has been done to them. Let's start with the purpose of a support system and what it is made of. We are going to dive a little deeper and add some guides for scapegoats in relationships that we identified in chapter 5. Here is what supportive relationships are made of.

1. Individuals in your life you can call on for empathetic, nonjudgmental, and loving advice when you need it.
2. Someone to talk to you and share your worries, victories, and your goals with. They will worry with you, celebrate with you, and encourage you.
3. They make time for you just like you make time for them. The relationship is mutual. There is take and give from both sides.

Another barrier scapegoats face when creating a support system is not knowing how to be vulnerable. The scapegoat has always been the one to take on the shame and then walk away. The scapegoat does not know how to unload the shame they feel and then stick around and enjoy dinner together. This is very uncomfortable for the scapegoat. They are more comfortable being the helper, the listener, and the one to show empathy. They do not know how to open up and just share what they are going through. Not knowing how to be vulnerable in a healthy way causes them to be vulnerable in unhealthy ways. They attract those that use them and do not give in return.

If you are a scapegoat, you will know how it feels when you try to open up to someone who you have always supported. It is almost like they will be speechless and then offer up some shame to you and then they change the subject. They do exactly what has been done to you in the past. They shame you and then send you away. In these moments, the relationship is very clear to us just how one-sided and unfair it is. Yet, somehow that does not keep us from coming back for more. We have to learn from the start of a new relationship what to look for and what to attach ourselves to. Once we "sign" up for a relationship with someone, it is very difficult to "sign out." We don't want a long list of ex-friends or broken relationships. We can avoid this by being more selective upfront with those we choose to enter into relationships with. Let's look at some traits of someone who is more likely to be a good support to us.

1. They remember a need you have, and they may act on it. Let's say you're speaking with a coworker, and you let them know you are out of markers and you need to remember to grab some from the supply room next time. After lunch, you notice a pack of markers on your desk. You go to the coworker and they say, "I was grabbing paper so I thought I would grab makers for you." This can feel like a BRAND-NEW experience. This person listened to your need and did not judge, shame, or ignore it. On top of that, they followed through and helped you

out. This person saw you, heard you, and went the extra mile to try to make your life a little less difficult. This is a trait of someone who could be a good support for you.

2. They check in with you. Someone that you shared something difficult with that follows up to see how you are doing or how it is going can be good support for you.

3. They do not shame you when you open up and talk about something you feel guilty or ashamed about. Instead, they hear you out and show you comfort. They may empathize with you or just let you know they are sad to hear that you are going through a hard time and let you know they are there for you. They do not use what you just told them to beat you over the head with and get you to feel small. They are sad with you.

4. They do not try to control you or abandon you. As a scapegoat, you were either neglected or controlled. Told what to say, where to go, or where not to go. How to dress, how to eat, how to walk, how and what to feel, and on and on. You were either controlled or you were abandoned. Someone who has what it takes to be a good support will not leave a voicemail tearing you down or threatening you for not answering their phone call. They will not guilt or manipulate you into doing what they want you to do. They won't tell you what you "should" do and then treat you poorly when you don't do it. However, they will also call and reach out to you. They will invite you to do things and also do things you want to do. There will be ebb and flow. They won't "ditch" you when new plans come up. If they know you are alone, they will invite you to join in on their plans. This

is not every time, but the point is, they will show you care. Just like you show care to them.

5. They initiate contact as well. They invite you to do things with them as well as accept your invitation. If you are always the one to initiate contact, they may not be available to be a support to you.

6. They do not put you down in public or in private.

It is common for scapegoats to think, "It's okay, I'm okay being the one to get us together I don't mind." It is important to remember that this may be the status of the relationship for the entire relationship. This is not a supportive relationship, it is a one-way-ship and eventually you will be drained, frustrated, and alone. The bigger issue is, you will continue to maintain the other toxic relationships in your life as well. Once you develop a support system, it gives you the strength to begin setting boundaries with those that shame and use you.

Going back to victimizing. We want to learn to share our experiences without looking for someone to validate our innocence.

We will know we are people-pleasing or seeking validation if we are running someone's name into the ground. We need to learn to share our experience without making someone "the bad guy." This is important for us to learn in order for us to leave our scapegoat role. We were singled out and turned into a bad guy somewhere in our past and this aided in our becoming a scapegoat. It was done to us and now we try to get out of being a scapegoat by doing it to someone else. When we do this, we end up becoming that bad guy when we shame and victimize someone else, regardless if it is the truth or not. We need to learn to speak our truth without running someone's name into the ground and casting shame on someone. This is very difficult especially when you are being victimized. We can, however, share our story without making someone the worst person on the planet. Let's look at an example.

Being the family scapegoat; Mark has been hit, stolen from, shamed, ignored, screamed at, lied about, and guilted. This happened anytime he became fed up and tried to stop the abusive treatment. The members of his family are not going to be able to see Mark any differently than the scapegoat image his mother has created for him, at least not for the time being. Mark is beginning to understand what he has gone through and now he is attempting to create a new support system.

However, each time he tries to explain what happened to him, he either ends up enraged and embarrasses himself, or he walks away feeling pathetic. These experiences are keeping him closed off and this prevents him from being able to create a healthy support system. In order to truly get out of this scapegoat role, scapegoats will need to learn how to develop a healthy, loving, and a mutual support system. Support systems give us the strength to stop accepting poor behavior, and they make it easier to let go and move on. Here is a new way for Mark to share his experience so someone can get to know him. This is how he can share his experience and what he faces every time his family comes up.

Mark- (Sharing with new supportive friend Steve that he has learned to trust) I'm thinking of not going home for Thanksgiving this year.

Steve- Really? How come?

Mark- My family has not always been the most respectful of me, and I have had a lot of hurt from them. I am thinking about stepping away for a bit, so I can clear my head and think. I do worry about what they will do if I skip Thanksgiving.

Steve- Oh I am sorry; I didn't know that. That's too bad and it sounds painful. What do you worry they will do? My family would say, "Oh okay see you at Christmas" and it would be no big deal, so this is new to me.

Mark- Well, I used to just do what they wanted me to in order to keep the peace. I am just really sick of the poor treatment. I am not totally sure what I worry about, I guess mostly guilt trips and they will want to punish me when and if I ever do come around again.

Steve- Wow, that sounds really unhealthy. It's like it won't stop regardless of what you do. You are an adult and you can make your own decisions. If anyone treats you poorly, you have a right to step away, family or not.

Mark- It's like I know that logically, but I almost feel programmed into not exercising my rights. To be honest, when I think about telling them no and that I am not coming I almost feel like I am going to die or something really bad is going to happen to me.

Steve- That sounds terrible! I'm really glad you are sharing this with me. I had no idea that this is what you go through with your family.

Notice how Mark shared his story and said what had been done to him and what he was going through without making someone the bad guy. He is still the victim of poor treatment, but he did not enter into that scapegoat role while sharing. He avoided this by not pointing out how "bad" someone was. If Mark had said, "My mom is such a liar. She's a terrible, evil, and manipulative person. She pins my brothers against me, so she can control me. She ruined my life and she won't stop until I'm back living with her again. My mother is the most hateful person I know. She is scary and not someone you would want to cross. She has treated me poorly my entire life. I cannot stand her!" All of this may be true as well, but we can see from reading both conversations that one is from a place of fear and panic and one is empowering. Remember, we maintain that scapegoat role when we run someone else's name into the ground and try to make them the bad guy.

Practice telling your story. Write it down and try to get it down to two or three lines. Look it over and if your story has a bad guy, try to write it again and again until it is concise and no one is being vilified. This stuff is hard. That is why we have some practice runs before we try to share it with someone else. Overall, the goal is to develop a system that supports you. This gives you the strength to say no more to those in your life that want to scapegoat you so they can feel better about their own shame. That is not your job. You were not born to be a scapegoat. You are a person with needs, wants, and goals. It is your life. You decide what you want to do with it. Next, let's look at how we can begin to live our lives.

Chapter 8

Stand Firm-Move On

Moving on can be scary. Change can be exciting, but it can also be intimidating. In the process of moving forward we can reminisce about the "good old" times. We can find that **one time** the person who scapegoats us was kind to us. However big or small their kind act was, we can hang on to that even if it was months or years ago. The event may have happened early on in the relationship, or there may have been kind acts few or far between. These single or few moments are the ones that pull at our heart strings and make us afraid to let go. Scapegoats are used to poor treatment, so when they receive kind treatment, they tend to hang on to it. When we take a step back, we realize in the scheme of things, the act or those few acts are not enough. They do not constitute a healthy relationship. There is nothing to miss. Someone who treats you well one or two times a year, if that, may not be someone you really even miss once you heal and move on from them. Especially when you free yourself up to be around people who respect you and are kind to you more often than not.

This is where the idea of standing firm comes into play. Standing firm in your initial decision to set boundaries and to hold them is what helps us to heal. It seems it is more common for us to return to our abusers than it is to make the decision to leave and never look back. We look back on those few kind moments and then we romanticize them and ultimately return. We do not want to return. When a scapegoat returns, it tends to be much worse for them. Setting boundaries into place is the beginning stages of standing firm. Here is an example of what a boundary may look like.

Mark has made the decision to step away from his family in an effort to create some distance so he can think. Mark realizes that every time James calls him, he has a panic attack and then gives into James' demands. Mark has learned, he cannot speak with James on the phone *and* stand his ground. In learning this, Mark has decided to set a boundary and will no longer speak with James on the phone. Mark will only communicate through text. This helps Mark to stay firm in his moving on process. Here is an example of how he holds this new boundary he has set.

James is calling Mark on the phone. Rather than answering it, Mark sends James a text. This is their conversation, all done through texts.

Mark- Hey James. I cannot talk right now, can you text?

James- Just call me when you get a second

Mark- I am not sure when that will be, it is better for me if you text

James- I do not like to text, just call when you are free

Here is the point where Mark is either going to acquiesce and call his brother and risk getting sucked back in, or he is going to stand firm. Mark decides James is the one who wants to tell him something and if it is important enough, he will text. He decides that he will not be calling James, but is open to texting with him. This is Mark standing firm and not returning to his role of scapegoat. James is not going to like Mark setting and holding a boundary. There may be some push back from him. He may try to punish Mark or use a smear campaign to get him back into alignment. This brings us to the next portion of this chapter…Moving On.

In the past, if Mark had decided to try and stand firm and set a boundary, he may have become afraid and then allowed the fear to consume him. The fear of what others would think and say about him would force him to run back for more punishment and control. However, Mark is beginning to find his strength. He is committed to refusing to accept punishment. He is not working hard to avoid punishment any longer. Mark now refuses to be around those that want to punish and control him. Mark now focuses on how he is being treated, rather than what he may or may not do to try to avoid punishment. Remember scapegoats are not shamed because of their actions, they are shamed because someone refuses to deal with their own shame. It does not matter what the scapegoat does, they will be treated poorly and blamed for it regardless. The only way the poor treatment would stop, is if the person in their lives would deal with their own shame. This is why scapegoats have to stand firm and keep moving on. The way they are treated is not up to them, they have to decide if they are willing to continue being punished or if they have had enough and move on.

Mark has decided to move on and will continue to push and move forward. He is refusing to sit and worry about the smear campaigns and the death seeds that have been used as tactics against him in the past. Mark instead focuses on the truth. When the toxic guilt flares up, he reminds himself, "I have done nothing wrong. It is not wrong for me to stay away from those that treat me poorly. It is wrong for others to treat me poorly and demand I keep secrets, carry the shame, and be their scapegoat. I wish them all the best, but for now I need to keep moving on and keep moving forward on my healing journey." Mark has developed this mantra that he repeats to himself any time he starts to doubt his decision to have boundaries. This helps to maintain the progress he has made and to continue to move forward.

Once boundaries have been implemented, two things can happen.

1. The people in your life will respect your boundaries and you can continue to move forward in peace with respect.
2. The people in your life will be offended by your boundaries and push back against them and attempt to punish you.

For those that push back and punish you, you may have to set a stronger boundary. I am hoping that by now you are a little more familiar with what the punishments look like. This is the smear campaign. The withholding of attention or affection, or it could be raging on you physically or verbally, and dumping heaps of toxic shame on you. The punishments are an effort to take down your boundaries and get you back into your role of scapegoat. When it becomes clear to you that this is not going to stop with the boundaries you have attempted to implement, you can do something called- going no contact. No contact means having zero interaction with the people who demand you stay a scapegoat. You do not look them up on social media, text, email, talk, or visit them. You do not have someone else fill you in on what they are doing in their lives. You have no contact with them.

This can be impossible if you are co-parenting with someone. You will need to have contact with the other parent on some level. You can consult with an attorney and decide the best way to limit the amount of access the other parent has to you. Some people have a court order that all contact is only done through a mediator. Others get a court order that all correspondence can only be about the child and must be done through email. Even if you are co-parenting there are steps you can take to safeguard yourself for better mental health. You do not have to be at the mercy of the person scapegoating you just because you share a child together. There are measures you can take; you may need to get an attorney involved.

Going no contact is a big decision to make. It could mean you losing contact with everyone that your tormentor is connected to. This can include family and or friends you will have to give up to escape your scapegoat role. Not all of your family or friends may go along with the smear campaigns and down play the punishment or the abuse. At the end of the day, you may find that you do not have to give up everyone your tormentor is associated with. Remember, the line is drawn in the sand at the point where someone expects, guilts, or demands that you accept punishment. Someone who shames you for having boundaries is not healthy for you. They may be a great person and just not understand because of their own shame. If this is someone you can talk to, you can try explaining to them why they are out of line in telling you what to do. If they chose not to respect your choices, you may have to limit contact with them or decide to go no contact whatsoever.

Going no contact can be super scary. In the past, not jumping at your tormentor's calling may have resulted in extreme punishment. There is also that death seed that comes into play. The death seed has the greatest impact when you are trying to set and hold boundaries. Once the boundary is set, you can begin to fear your tormentor's death. The worry of how you are going to feel when they die along with all of the other fears associated with their death from Chapter 6. Now we go back to the stand firm portion of this chapter. This is where you hold your boundaries and reach out to your support system.

Someone who has not been scapegoated is not going to understand the depths and the extent of the psychological warfare that goes on inside of a person who was scapegoated. They just will not. Being scapegoated is so unnatural. A scapegoat reading this is going to know exactly what I am talking about in a way that someone who was not scapegoated is never going to understand.

Scapegoats get both sides of the shameful field. They may hear things like, "Why would you put up with that, just tell them to get lost and move on", or "How could you not talk to your mom? That's your mom. Don't you feel bad, she's old." So much has to be factored in and picked apart when making the decision to go no contact or to limit contact. There are people in your life that are not going to understand. The alternative is to stay and continue getting scapegoated. Most scapegoats live in fear of what will be done to them if they stay and they are also afraid of what will be done to them if they leave. Sometimes the fear of leaving is greater than the fear of staying. I am not able or going to make that decision for you. This is a decision we all have to make for ourselves. Most times, making this decision is a process.

Scapegoats were not taught to leave; they were sent away and then summoned when needed. Leaving is a foreign concept. Leaving is something that people with rights get to do. I assure you; you too have the right to leave. Remember, we do not get our rights by waiting for someone to give them to us. We already have our rights; we just need to exercise them. If you decide to leave, stop talking to someone, stop returning texts or phone calls, that is your right. As an adult if you choose to do that, it is your right. You decide who you speak with and who you let into your life. That choice is yours and it is your right to make it. It is your business and no one else's. Now that we have gone a little more in depth on limiting contact and going no contact, let's look now at how to embrace the life you want.

Chapter 9

Learning to Embrace a Toxic Guilt-Free Life

As you begin to wake up and understand what has happened to you, one thing you may discover is you do not know what to do with your life. This new freedom you are finding may cause you to want to return to the punishment. Not being shamed, controlled, and punished can feel strange. I hope you get to a place where you **hate** feeling punished. Where you refuse to tolerate it. When we do something bad then feeling guilty is good. We need to feel guilty for the wrongs we commit so we can make amends and do better next time. What we do not need is someone trying to use guilt on us in an effort to control us. This is not guilt, remember this is toxic guilt and we cannot allow that to control us.

After being scapegoated for so long, you may be completely unaware of who you really are. Now is your time. It's your time to live and discover what moves you, what you love, and to make your space your own. Scapegoats are trained to wait on someone else. We wait for them to tell us what we should be eating, doing and how we should be spending our time and money. What our space should look like. It is important to make your life your own. Allow yourself to dream and to dream big.

Use the following prompts to explore who you are.

1. Where would I love to live and why?
2. What is my favorite part of my home or my space and why?
3. Which area of my space would I love to make more of my own?
4. Does my space reflect who I am? Does it represent my interests, hobbies, and what brings me comfort? If yes how, and if no why not?
5. If I could change something about my space, what would it be?
6. What are three things that I value? For example, what draws me towards it the most? Some examples may be: family, animals, health, stability, education, relationships, books, etc.
7. How can I bring my values into my space, so my space can more accurately reflect who I am? For example, if I value relationships, do I have pictures on my walls of those I have relationships with? If you value learning, do you have a bookcase with books? If you love walking into a home with lots of plants, do you have any? If you value stability and you live in chaos, then your space would not be reflecting what you value.

This was an exercise to get you thinking about your space. What more do you wish to look at? How about the clothes you wear? Do the clothes you wear reflect who you are as a person or do you want to change them? Your car. What type of car do you like? Do you like SUVs, minivans, sedans… What type of car do you love versus what type of car do you drive? Does your car reflect who you are? This is not being shallow. This is about you taking ownership of your life and the way you are living. Learning how to be in charge of your life and not feeling toxic guilt about it. Not being worried about what ANYONE has to say about it. It is your life. Others are living *their life,* and you get to live *yours.*

Scapegoats need to go through a reconnecting period. It won't always be like this. Over time, once you get to know yourself better and you begin making some changes and living your life, it will become second nature. Not only that, but when someone comes along and tries to lay some toxic guilt on you, it will be very obvious what they are doing and you won't fall for it anymore. Life will no longer revolve around you trying to prove you are good. Your behavior and decisions will no longer be driven or influenced by the possibility of someone accusing you of being bad. Life will now be based on what you want and how you want to live.

It is shocking how much time you have to live your life and do things that you enjoy doing when you are no longer someone's scapegoat. You have a whole life to live now. You have 8,760 hours every year. They are your hours to spend. Do some math if you want to. Add up the time you have given to your tormentors. You have 24 hours in a day and 7 days in a week. That adds up to about 720 hours per month. Times either of those numbers by the number of weeks/months you have already given your tormentors to get *your* number. You can also times 8,760 for every year you have been their scapegoat. If you have been the scapegoat for 3 years, then you have given them 26,280 of your hours.

How many hours is it for you? Is that enough? Have you given them enough of your hours yet? If not, how many hours do you feel you owe them? When will it be enough? Remember, you are in charge of what you do during those hours. It is not just about not doing things you hate or dread. It is about doing what you *love*. Spending your time with those who value you and appreciate your efforts. It's about not wasting time in general and especially not wasting your time on those that abuse you and treat you as though you are their scapegoat. You are no one's scapegoat. It is not your job to be the secret keeper. You are a person that deserves a great life that is filled with the things and the people you love. Stop doing things you hate and start living a life you love.

Once you decide to stop being a scapegoat, and especially if you put some boundaries in place, you may have people within the system reach out to you. You may suddenly find distant relatives wanting to talk or inviting you to events. This can be for a number of different reasons. If you decide to interact with them, please put some boundaries in place for yourself before you meet up. Remember, all of your experiences are your story and you do not owe them to anyone. You decide if you feel safe with someone and then you decide if and how much of your story you wish to share. The system or person will want their scapegoat back. Without you around they will be confronted with their shame. Do not get sucked back in. It will be with future promises, toxic guilt, or even the death of a loved one. Remember the hours you have already given them, is that not enough? Someone's inability to reflect your value and own their shameful behavior, has nothing to do with you or the person you are. You are worth more, you always were.

As we come to the end of the book, I want to thank you for taking this journey with me. I know that this is a painful one. This burden of the scapegoat is real and because of all the manipulation that goes along with it, escaping it can mean having to leave so much behind. Own your life and give yourself permission to walk away from anyone that expects you to accept shame and punishment for someone else. Get your life. Embrace what you love and those that love you. Spend your hours where it matters. Refuse to give even one more hour to someone who expects you to accept poor treatment.

You my friend, are a scapegoat, no more, forever!

Reference

Bradshaw, John. (1988). *Healing the shame that binds you.* Health Communications, Inc.

Cukor, G. (Director). (1944). *Gaslight* [Film]. Metro-Goldwyn-Mayer.

Wegscheider-Cruse, S. (1981). *Another chance: Hope & health for the alcoholic family.* Palo Alto, Calif: Science and Behavior Books.

Made in United States
Troutdale, OR
12/07/2023